Totally WACKY FACTS ABOUT LAND ANIMALS

CARI MEISTER

raintree

a Capstone company — publishers for children

WATCH OUT! A group of rhinos is called a

CRASH.

THE CHICKEN IS CLOSELY RELATED TO TYRANNOSAURUS REX.

GREAT UNCLE T.

Why didn't I get those **HUGE TEETH?**

A chicken has a **COMB** on its head and two **WATTLES** under its neck.

Mike the Headless Chicken lived for 18 months without **HIS HEAD!**

Baby monkeys suck their THUMBS.

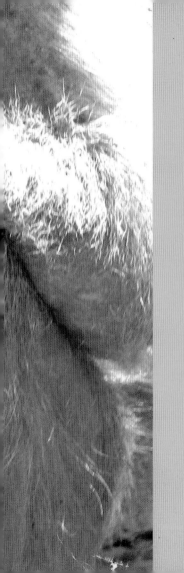

Baby elephants suck their TRUNKS.

Giraffes use their **TONGUES** to clean their **EARS** and **NOSES**.

Orangutans use their **teeth** to clip their **toenails.**

Pet cats spend 50% of their waking time GROOMING THEMSELVES.

11

SLOTHS POO ONLY ONCE A WEEK.

I should try **EATING BAMBOO!**

SOME HUMMINGBIRDS WEIGH LESS THAN A PENNY.

A bumblebee bat is the world's smallest mammal. It's as heavy as TWO PAPERCLIPS.

The world's smallest dog, a **chihuahua**, can fit inside a POCKET.

1 SECOND:

THE TIME IT TAKES A TIGER BEETLE TO RUN 120 TIMES ITS OWN BODY LENGTH

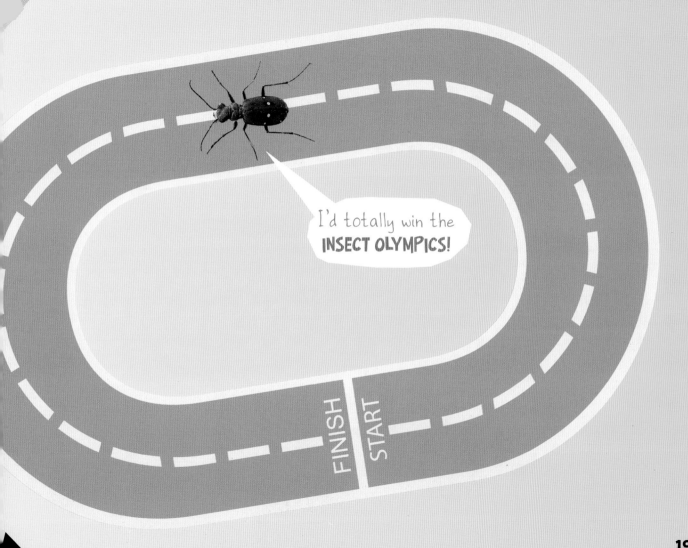

The cheetah clocks in as the **fastest mammal,** running 110 kilometres (70 miles) per hour.

The **PEREGRINE FALCON** can reach speeds of up to

322 KILOMETRES (200 miles) **PER HOUR!**

Pit vipers can see INFRARED.

22

Rats have an uncanny ability to DETECT LAND MINES.

The greater wax moth can hear sounds at higher frequencies than any other animal.

And you thought I was A PEST?

23

The African drongo bird mimics a meerkat's warning call to steal MEERKAT FOOD.

A hawk moth caterpillar larva looks like **A SNAKE** to fool predators.

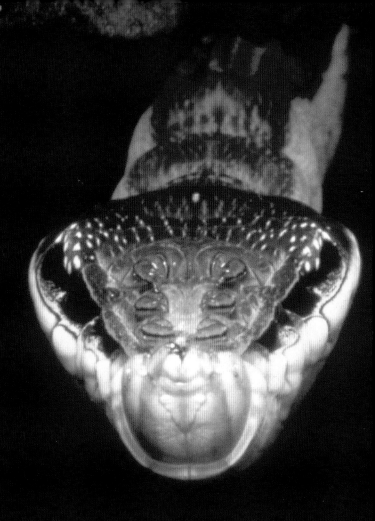

Male "dancing frogs" WAVE THEIR LEGS in the air to ATTRACT FEMALES.

A FEMALE SLUG sometimes bites off a male slug's **PRIVATE PARTS.**

Seriously?
AHHHH!

Male porcupines **WEE** on females before **mating.**

HOGNOSE SNAKES

let out stinky "**death**" smells to avoid CAPTURE.

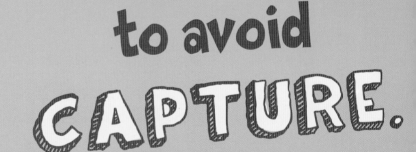

SOME DUCKS PLAY DEAD TO AVOID BECOMING A FOX'S MEAL.

An opossum will PLAY DEAD for hours, even sticking out its tongue for added effect.

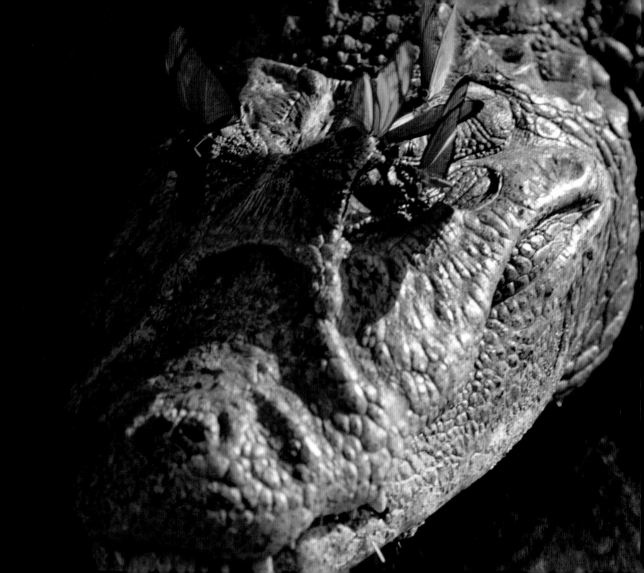

Bees and butterflies drink CROCODILE TEARS.

SOME MOTHS HAVE HARPOON-SHAPED MOUTHPARTS TO SUCK TEARS FROM SLEEPING BIRDS.

Some kinds of carpenter ants purposely explode with TOXIC GOO to stop predators.

The Moroccan flic-flac spider BACKFLIPS to get away from its enemies.

CATCH ME
if you can!

HIPPOS FLING POO AT EACH OTHER WHEN GETTING OUT OF THE WATER.

Flies lay their eggs in rotting flesh.

A JACKAL CUB EATS ITS MUM'S VOMIT.

TUSKS ARE REALLY VERY LARGE TEETH.

An elephant's tusks can grow to be 3 metres (10 feet) long.

A cow's udder can hold almost **23 LITRES** (6 gallons) of milk.

Got an **upset stomach?** Try drinking

MOOSE MILK!

Dropping a frog into milk will keep the milk **FRESH.**

An alligator tooth can regrow 50 TIMES.

A vulture VOMITS to keep enemies at bay.

FLIES EAT POO.

THE EMPEROR TAMARIN MONKEY HAS A LONG, BUSHY, WHITE MOUSTACHE!

You **KNOW** you want one too!

A zebra's stripes keep biting flies AWAY.

47

WANT TO HAVE A SNOWBALL FIGHT? JAPANESE MACAQUE MONKEYS WILL JOIN YOU!

Millions of **monarch butterflies** migrate to the Monarch Butterfly Reserve in Mexico each autumn. Trees there **BEND** with the weight of all of the butterflies!

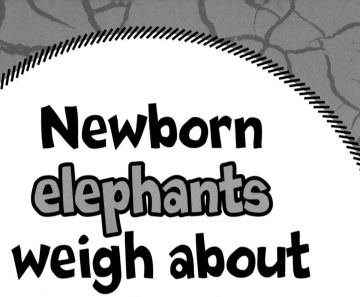

Newborn elephants weigh about 91 KILOGRAMS (200 pounds)!

A newborn hippo can weigh 50 KILOGRAMS (110 pounds).

EGYPTIAN VULTURES USE
ROCKS TO BREAK OPEN
OSTRICH EGGS.

The American burying beetle buries dead birds and rodents for its **BABIES** to eat.

Flamingos eat with their heads UPSIDE DOWN.

ELEPHANTS ARE THE ONLY LAND MAMMALS THAT CAN'T JUMP.

A penguin can't fly, but it can JUMP 2 metres (6 ft) in the air from the water!

The Australian striped rocket frog can jump over 1.2 METRES (4 FT).

Kangaroos can't run, but they can travel 8 metres (25 ft) IN ONE LEAP.

THINK FARM ANIMALS ARE BORING?

MUSIC CALMS NERVOUS COWS.

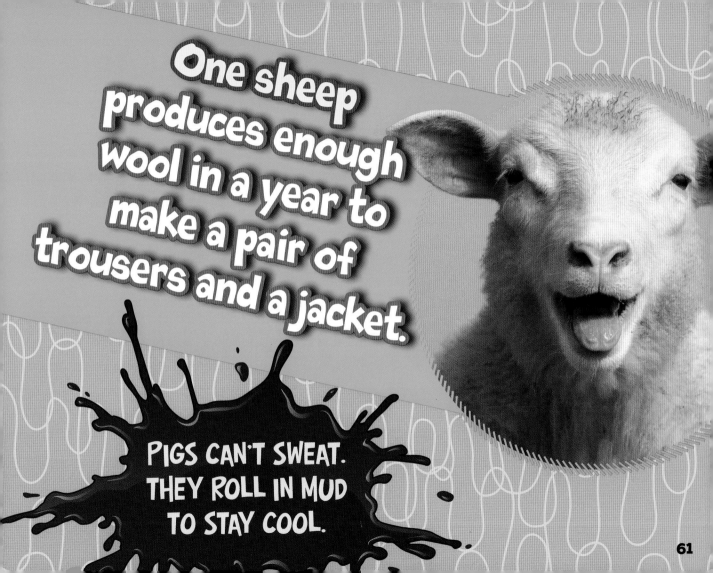

One sheep produces enough wool in a year to make a pair of trousers and a jacket.

PIGS CAN'T SWEAT. THEY ROLL IN MUD TO STAY COOL.

61

A dog called Chaser has learned to recognize more than 1,000 words.

CROWS MAY BE ABLE TO COUNT.

1, 2, 3...

SOME ELEPHANTS CAN BE TRAINED TO PAINT SELF-PORTRAITS.

Rhino horns are made up of the same stuff as your HAIR.

THE NAKED MOLE RAT HAS NO HAIR.

Monkeys pick (and eat) INSECTS out of each other's hair.

POLAR BEAR MOTHERS GAIN **181 KILOGRAMS (400 POUNDS)** DURING PREGNANCY.

Mama crocodiles carry their babies around in their MOUTHS.

The yellow ant smells like a **LEMON.**

One type of millipede smells like **CHERRY COLA.**

The hoatzin bird smells like **COW DUNG.**

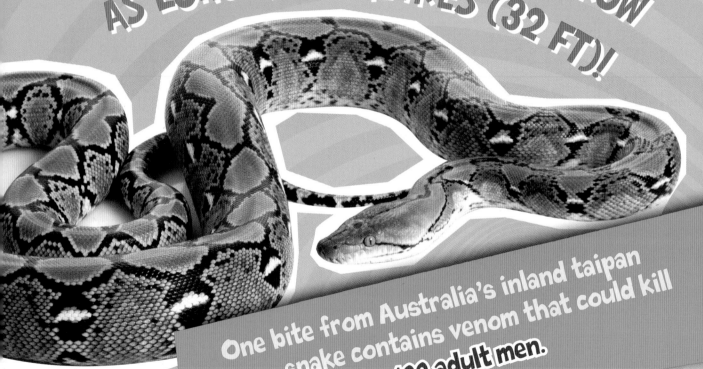

RETICULATED PYTHONS CAN GROW AS LONG AS 10 METRES (32 FT)!

One bite from Australia's inland taipan snake contains venom that could kill **100 adult men.**

MANY SNAKES DISLOCATE THEIR JAWS SO THEY CAN SWALLOW LARGE ANIMALS WHOLE.

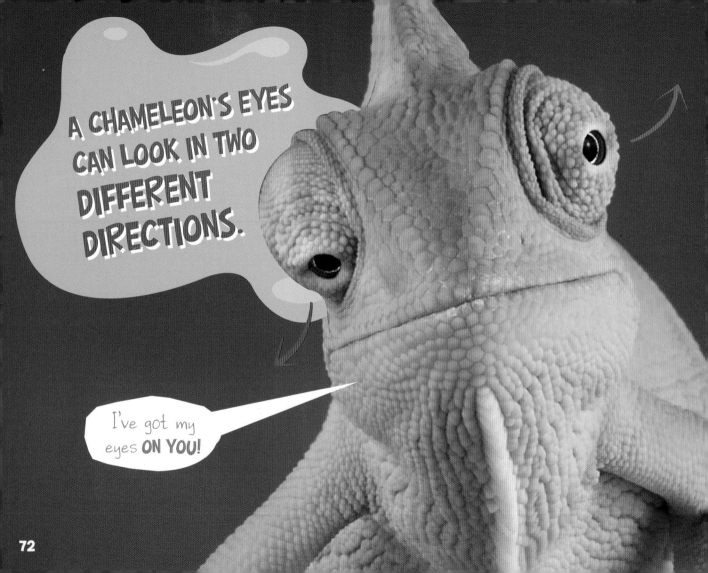

The horned lizard can shoot **BLOOD** out of its eyes.

SNAKES DO NOT BLINK.

natural sunscreen droplet

A HIPPO'S SWEAT ACTS AS A SUNSCREEN AND INSECT REPELLENT.

Geckos can REGROW their tails.

If a flatworm is **cut in half,** each piece will grow into a **new worm.**

TWO DAYS AFTER AN ANT DIES, OTHER ANTS CARRY IT AWAY TO AN ANT GRAVEYARD.

RHINOS COVER
THEMSELVES IN MUD
TO KEEP INSECTS AWAY.

Polar bears have **BLACK SKIN.**

Like its fur, a tiger's skin is **STRIPED.**

A BALD EAGLE'S NEST CAN BE MORE THAN 2.7 METRES (9 FT) ACROSS AND 6 METRES (20 FT) OFF THE GROUND.

An edible-nest swiftlet makes its nest out of **SPIT.**

SOCIABLE WEAVERS BUILD MASSIVE NESTS THAT HOUSE 400 BIRDS.

Female American sand burrowing mayflies live for less than 5 minutes.

GALAPAGOS TORTOISES CAN LIVE TO BE 150 YEARS OLD.

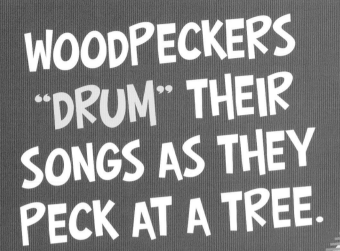

WOODPECKERS "DRUM" THEIR SONGS AS THEY PECK AT A TREE.

HOUSEFLIES HUM IN THE KEY OF F!

A red-eyed vireo sings 20,000 songs per day.

That's more songs than you have on **YOUR MP3 PLAYER!**

Giraffes sleep with their eyes HALF OPEN.

HORSES, ZEBRAS AND ELEPHANTS SLEEP STANDING UP.

A CAT'S EAR HAS **32 MUSCLES**;
A HUMAN'S EAR HAS **2.**

100,000: the number of muscles in an elephant's trunk

OWLS SWALLOW
THEIR FOOD WHOLE
AND THEN COUGH UP
PELLETS OF BONES
AND FUR.

Blister beetles release a chemical used to treat **human warts.**

1,000: THE NUMBER OF MOSQUITOES A BAT CAN EAT IN AN HOUR

Insects have been on Earth for about 400 million years.

A type of skink lizard has

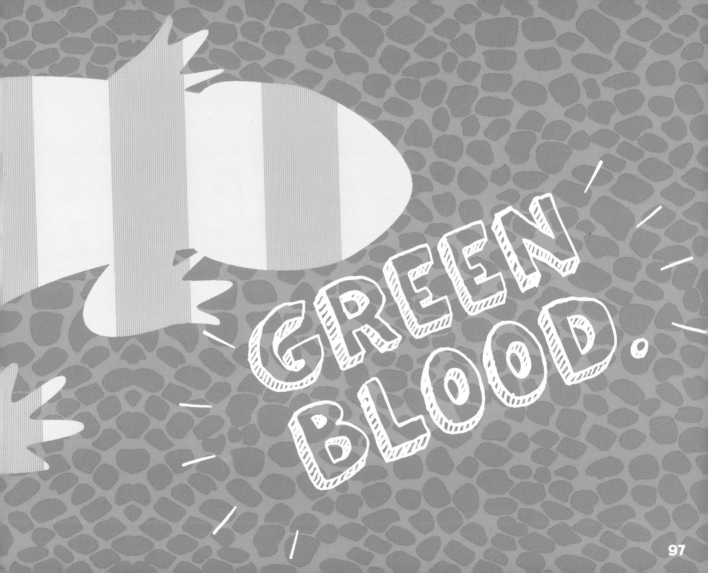

GREEN BLOOD.

A millipede can have up to 750 legs.

A CATERPILLAR HAS 16 LEGS.

Most
spiders have
four sets
of eyes.

A TARSIER'S EYE IS **BIGGER** THAN ITS BRAIN.

DRAGONFLIES HAVE 360-DEGREE VISION.

I CAN SEE YOU!

Female mandrill monkeys like males with brightly coloured behinds and faces.

MALE FRIGATE BIRDS INFLATE THEIR HUGE, RED NECK POUCH TO ATTRACT FEMALES.

A chipmunk's cheek pouches can hold about 32 beech nuts.

A mole can dig a tunnel that's 90 metres (300 ft) long in about 20 HOURS.

ONE UNDERGROUND PRAIRIE DOG BURROW COVERED  65,000 SQUARE KILOMETRES (25,000 SQUARE MILES)!

THERE ARE **TWO** SPECIES OF ELEPHANTS IN THE WORLD.

FOUR TYPES OF ANTEATERS EXIST.

THERE ARE **EIGHT** TYPES OF BEARS.

THERE ARE **400,000** SPECIES OF BEETLES.

AND MORE THAN **1.5 MILLION** TYPES OF INSECTS HAVE BEEN NAMED IN THE WORLD!

GLOSSARY

chemical substance used in or made by chemistry; chemistry is the study of the way substances combine and react with one another

frequency number of sound waves that pass a location in a certain amount of time

harpoon barbed spear used to hunt large fish

infrared one of the colours of the light spectrum that we cannot see

land mine explosive device laid on or just beneath the surface of the ground

mammal warm–blooded animal that breathes air; mammals have hair or fur; female mammals feed milk to their young

migrate move from one place to another

mimic copy

pellet mass of undigested hair, fur and bones vomited up by an owl or other bird of prey

predator animal that hunts other animals for food

repellent substance that is able to keep something away

species group of animals with similar features

uncanny beyond what is normal or expected

venom poisonous liquid produced by some animals

wattle extra skin that hangs from the head or neck

READ MORE

Amazing Animal Movers (Animal Superpowers), John Townsend (Raintree, 2013)

Animal Infographics (Infographics), Chris Oxlade (Raintree, 2015)

SuperNature (DK Nature), Derek Harvey (Dorling Kindersley, 2012)

WEBSITES

www.bbc.co.uk/nature/collections/p00hldcc
Discover facts about nature's record breakers.

www.guinnessworldrecords.com
Learn about interesting world records and watch amazing video clips.

INDEX

Raintree is an imprint of Capstone Global Library Limited, a company incorporated in England and Wales having its registered office at 7 Pilgrim Street, London, EC4V 6LB – Registered company number: 6695582

www.raintree.co.uk
myorders@raintree.co.uk

Edited by Shelly Lyons
Designed by Aruna Rangarajan
Picture research by Svetlana Zhurkin
Creative Director Nathan Gassman
Production by Lori Barbeau

ISBN 978 1 4747 0588 2
19 18 17 16 15
10 9 8 7 6 5 4 3 2 1

British Library Cataloguing in Publication Data
A full catalogue record for this book is available from the British Library.

Every effort has been made to contact copyright holders of material reproduced in this book. Any omissions will be rectified in subsequent printings if notice is given to the publisher.

Printed in China.

Acknowledgements
Dreamstime: Daniel Caluian, 43, Joan Egert, 16 (left), P L, 3, Peter Bjerregaard, 89; Getty Images: Claus Meyer, 30—31, Dante Fenolio, 25, David M. Schleser, 29, Merlin D. Tutle, 17 (top), The LIFE Picture Collection/Bob Landry, 7 (right); Minden Pictures: Mark Moffett, 26, Masahiro Iijima, Nature Production, 54, Vincent Grafhorst, 34; Shutterstock: abeadev, 7 (left), Abraham Badenhorst, 44—45, Adam Gryko, 39 (frog), agongallud, 109 (top), Alice Mary Herden, 6 (right), Amesan, 91, ANCH, 90, Andy Dean Photography, 5, Apostrophe, 102, Bildagentur Zoonar GmbH, 106, bluedarkat, 4 (bottom), BlueRingMedia, 66 (bottom), bumihills, 63, Caroline Devulder, 109 (back), Cathy Keifer, 72, CyberKat, 21, Dayna More, 100 (right), dedMazay, 78, Dr. Morley Read, 92—93, Edwin Verin, 100 (left), egg design, 27, elnavegante, 16 (right), Eric Isselee, 37, 41, 62, fivespots, 70, Frank Wasserfuehrer, 103, Gualberto Becerra, cover (top right), Hung Chung Chih, 14 (right), Iakov Filimonov, 66 (top), ingret, 11, JGade, cover (top left), Jo Crebbin, 13, John Michael Evan Potter, 83, Jon Beard, 47, koi88, 60, koosen, 17 (bottom), Kuttelvaserova Stuchelova, 86, lendy16, 95 (front), LiliGraphie, 6 (frame), lineartestpilot, 68 (middle), Lisa Yen, 68 (right), lumen-digital, 53, Mackey Creations, 55 (left), makar, 88, mart, 64, Matt Jeppson, 76—77, Matthew Cole, 23 (left), Max Fat, 28, Maxi_m, 108 (right), mayakova, 69 (popcorn), Michael C. Gray, 99, Michael G. McKinne, 2, mountainpix, 74—75, Nagel Photography, 10, nattanan726, 15, Nikola m, 95 (mosquito), NinaM, 40, Noradoa, 50, panbazil (turkey), back cover, 4, panda3800, 4 (top right), PandaWild, 22 (left), pcnorth, 87, Peter Waters, 12, Philip Bird LRPS CPAGB, 80, Photo Africa, 55 (right), photobar, 20—21, photoiconix, 84—85, Radu Bercan, 94, reptiles4all, 22 (right), Robert Eastman, 6 (right), Ron Rowan Photography, 104, Rozhkovs, 42, Sarah2, 19 (top), schankz, 35, Sergio Schnitzler, 8, showcake, 39, Slanapotam, 18, Stephen Lew, 56—57, stockphoto mania, 69 (front), Terry234, 1 (back), 108 (left), Tom Bird, 61 (right), Tony Campbell, 82, tratong, 65, tsnebula23, 71, Vaclav Volrab, cover (bottom right), Vadim Petrakov, 14 (left), veroxdale, 59, Vital9cbl4, 19 (back), Volkova, cover (bottom left), 23 (right), voylodyon, 101, wawritto, 96—97, Yusak_P, 68 (left); SuperStock: age fotostock, 67, Steve Bloom Images, 49; Wikimedia: Ingo Rechenberg, 33

Design Elements by Capstone and Shutterstock

All the internet addresses (URLs) given in this book were valid at the time of going to press. However, due to the dynamic nature of the internet, some addresses may have changed, or sites may have changed or ceased to exist since publication. While the author and publisher regret any inconvenience this may cause readers, no responsibility for any such changes can be accepted by either the author or the publisher.